Psychology of Residential and Commercial Real Estate

Master the Psychology Behind Real Estate Success

By Willem Tait

Published by WRT Publishing

Copyright © 2024 by Willem Tait
All rights reserved.

No part of this publication may be reproduced, distributed, or transmitted in any form or by any means, including photocopying, recording, or other electronic or mechanical methods, without the prior written permission of the author, except in the case of brief quotations embodied in reviews and certain other noncommercial uses permitted by copyright law.

For permission requests, contact the author at:
willemtait@gmail.com or willemtait@outlook.com

This book is for educational and informational purposes only. The author is not liable for any damages or losses arising from the use or misuse of the content in this book.

Cover Design: Time Brands
Published by WRT Publishing

First Edition (2024)
Revised Edition (2025)
This edition includes updated formatting, new front and back matter, and added glossaries for psychology and real estate. It reflects the continued refinement of the author's work on the psychology behind residential and commercial real estate.

ISBN Print Library: 978-0-6398578-4-8
ISBN eBook Library: 978-0-6398578-5-5
ISBN Paperback Amazon KDP: 9798302727053
ISBN Hardcover Amazon KDP: 9798302728791

Why this book and why now?

Real estate runs on human judgment.
Not just rates and rentals.
People. Perception. Pressure.
That is the heart of this book.

You will see how first impressions tilt choices.
How emotion steers offers and timing.
How dissonance makes buyers and sellers defend bad calls.
How anchors set price in the mind.
How framing changes the same facts.
How trust forms and breaks.
How scarcity speeds action.
How social proof moves the crowd.
How heuristics save time and cause blind spots.
How hedonic adaptation dulls value.
How loss aversion blocks good exits.
How the endowment effect inflates worth.
How the status quo bias freezes decisions.
How sunk costs trap capital.

Each idea is explained in plain language.

Residential and commercial examples appear throughout.
Landlords, tenants, buyers, sellers, investors, and managers are all in view.
You get clear links between psychology and price, risk, and outcomes.

Why this book?
Because it maps the forces you face every week.
It shows where judgment bends.
It shows where margin leaks.
It shows how to spot the bend before it bends you.

Why now?
Markets are noisy.
Capital is cautious.
Attention is short.
In times like these, the edge is understanding how people actually decide.

Use these chapters to see more than the spreadsheet.
To read the room with fewer mistakes.
To time your asks with more care.
To price, position, and negotiate with a cleaner lens.

No hype.
No tricks.

Just a practical tour of the biases and effects that shape real deals.
So you can make better calls.
And help others do the same.

Turn the page.
Test one idea in your next meeting.
Then another in your next valuation.
Small shifts add up.
That is why this book.
That is why now.

Table of Contents

Why this book and why now? 2
Table of Contents 5
Introduction..7
CHAPTER 1: Perception Bias in Real Estate 9
CHAPTER 2: Emotional Decisions in Real Estate ...16
READERS NOTES..21
CHAPTER 3: Cognitive Dissonance in Real Estate.23
CHAPTER 4: Anchoring Bias in Real Estate............30
CHAPTER 5: Framing Effect in Real Estate 37
READERS NOTES..42
CHAPTER 6: Trust Building in Real Estate 44
CHAPTER 7: Scarcity Mindset in Real Estate..........51
READERS NOTES..56
CHAPTER 8: Social Proof in Real Estate 58
READERS NOTES..63
CHAPTER 9: Heuristic Thinking in Real Estate 65
CHAPTER 10: Hedonic Adaptation in Real Estate ..71
READERS NOTES..76
CHAPTER 11: Loss Aversion in Real Estate............78
CHAPTER 12: Endowment Effect in Real Estate 84
CHAPTER 13: Status Quo Bias in Real Estate.........90
CHAPTER 14: Sunk Cost Fallacy in Real Estate 96
READERS NOTES..101
CHAPTER 15: Book Summary and Conclusion.....103

Glossaries of Psychology and Real Estate............110
    Glossary of Psychological Concepts 111
    Glossary of Real Estate Concepts..................113
READERS NOTES...116
Updated List of Books to Date 117
    Real Estate Mastery Books Series 120
Acknowledgement..121
Author Bio 123
Social Profiles and Contact Info 125
Public Speaking, Mentorship, Consulting and Coaching 127
Upcoming Projects 129
We Value Your Feedback!..132
    Portfolio of Books by Willem Tait 139

Introduction

What happens when consumer psychology, real estate, investment and business collide? The result is a fascinating exploration of how human behavior shapes one of the most significant industries in the world.

Residential and commercial real estate isn't just about properties, it's about understanding people, their decisions, and the forces that drive them.

By examining this intersection, you can unlock new ways to navigate the market with clarity and confidence.

This book dives deep into the psychology behind real estate, revealing how biases and emotions influence decisions. From the urgency of the scarcity mindset to the grip of the sunk cost fallacy, these principles affect buyers, sellers, landlords, developers, and financiers alike. By understanding these dynamics, you'll gain tools to avoid costly mistakes and seize opportunities others might overlook.

Whether you're a landlord, a buyer, a seller, a tenant, a property manager, an investor, a banker, an evaluator, a property professional, an architect, a property developer, a quantity surveyor, or even a building contractor, you'll find value in this book. It offers practical examples and actionable insights to help you balance emotion with logic, recognize hidden opportunities, and make informed decisions in both residential and commercial markets.

Real estate is more than transactions, it's about people and their stories. By embracing the psychological aspects of the industry, you'll not only improve your strategies but also gain an edge in understanding the behaviors that drive the market.

Ready to uncover the secrets to mastering real estate through the lens of psychology?

Let this book be your guide.

CHAPTER 1: Perception Bias in Real Estate

Have you ever stepped into a property, residential or commercial, and felt an immediate pull, like it was the perfect fit? Maybe it was the way sunlight filtered through the windows of a home or the modern, open layout of a commercial office space that just seemed to scream productivity.

That first impression is often more powerful than we realise. It doesn't matter whether you're a landlord, buyer, seller, tenant, property manager, investor, bank evaluator, or property professional, perception bias influences everyone.

For residential buyers, the appeal of a cozy living room with a crackling fireplace might overshadow practical concerns like maintenance costs. Similarly, a tenant searching for a flat might prioritise how inviting the kitchen looks, even if the lease terms aren't ideal. On the commercial side, perception bias plays a massive role in decisions about office spaces, retail units, and warehouses. A brightly lit office with a sleek reception area can make a property manager or tenant overlook issues like limited parking or poor accessibility. These first impressions often dictate how the entire property is perceived from then on.

For landlords and property managers, this bias is an opportunity and a challenge.

In residential real estate, a freshly painted wall or a tidy garden can command higher rents. In commercial spaces, elements like polished floors, professional signage, or even just the smell of fresh paint can create the perception of a well-maintained, premium property. However, if these visual cues are absent, even the most functional spaces might be undervalued. The same applies to bank evaluators, who may unconsciously assign higher values to properties that simply "feel right."

Sellers, whether of homes or commercial properties, often fall victim to their own perception bias.

A homeowner might see their house as priceless, not because of its market value, but because of years of memories made within its walls. Meanwhile, the owner of a retail space might overvalue their property because it was their first big investment or because it previously housed a successful business. This emotional connection can make it harder for sellers to accept market realities, leading to drawn-out negotiations or missed opportunities.

In commercial real estate, developers and investors frequently use perception bias to their advantage. Think of high-end office buildings with glass facades and designer lobbies. These aren't just spaces for work, they're statements of success. For tenants, these features might overshadow practical concerns like higher rent or less square footage. Similarly, residential property developers know that a staged home with carefully selected furniture can evoke emotions that make buyers feel at home, even before they've made an offer.

Market trends are also shaped by perception bias. In residential areas, a trendy café or boutique gym opening nearby can change how people perceive the entire neighbourhood, driving up demand and property values. On the commercial side, the presence of anchor tenants like a well-known retail chain can elevate the appeal of an entire shopping centre. These external factors create a ripple effect that influences not only buyers and tenants but also landlords and investors evaluating potential opportunities.

Even for seasoned professionals like property managers and bank evaluators, perception bias can subtly sway decisions.

A retail space in a bustling location might seem more lucrative than it truly is because of its foot traffic, even if the tenant turnover rate is high. Similarly, a well-maintained home might appear more valuable to an evaluator than a larger but less polished one.

These biases can lead to misjudgments if not carefully managed.

As an investor, buyer, or tenant, it's crucial to recognise when perception bias might be clouding your judgment. Are you drawn to the aesthetics of a property more than its functionality?

As a landlord, property manager, or seller, are you leaning too heavily on the emotional or visual appeal of your property without addressing its underlying value? And as a bank evaluator or property professional, are you accounting for these psychological influences when assessing properties?

The balance between residential and commercial real estate often hinges on these subtle perceptions. A landlord renting out a modern loft in a vibrant city centre might focus on aesthetics to attract young professionals.

Meanwhile, a commercial property manager might prioritise the perceived prestige of their building to secure long-term corporate tenants. In both cases, understanding and leveraging perception bias is key to achieving success.

Chapter Conclusion and Call to Action

Perception bias is the invisible hand shaping decisions across residential and commercial real estate.

Whether you're a buyer, seller, tenant, landlord, property manager, investor, bank evaluator, or property professional, recognising the power of first impressions can give you an edge.

The next time you evaluate a property, whether it's a family home, an office, or a retail space, ask yourself:

"Am I seeing its true value, or am I influenced by what's on the surface?"

Awareness is the first step to making smarter, more balanced decisions. Let's reshape how we see real estate, one perception at a time.

READERS NOTES

CHAPTER 2: Emotional Decisions in Real Estate

Emotions are at the core of every decision we make, whether we realise it or not. In real estate, emotions often take the driver's seat, steering buyers, sellers, landlords, tenants, property managers, investors, and even banks toward choices that may not always align with logic.

From the joy of closing a deal to the frustration of unforeseen complications, emotions shape decisions in ways that can have lasting impacts on both business and personal lives.

For residential buyers, purchasing a home is rarely just a financial transaction, it's a deeply personal experience. The excitement of finding the "perfect" home can sometimes cloud practical considerations like affordability or long-term maintenance. A young couple might stretch their budget to buy a house with a dream kitchen, ignoring the fact that it's far from their workplace. Similarly, tenants often make emotional choices when selecting a rental property, prioritising features like natural light or a charming neighbourhood over the monthly rent they can realistically afford.

Sellers, too, are driven by emotions, particularly when it comes to letting go of a property with sentimental value. A homeowner might set an unrealistic asking price because they see the home as more than bricks and mortar, it's where they raised their family or celebrated milestones. This emotional attachment can lead to prolonged negotiations or even missed opportunities if buyers perceive the price as unjustified. Landlords, on the other hand, might hold onto a problematic tenant out of guilt or empathy, even when it hurts their bottom line.

In commercial real estate, emotions are equally influential, though they often manifest differently.

Investors might feel a rush of excitement when a new retail space or office block hits the market, pushing them to act quickly without fully assessing the risks. A property manager might prioritise a flashy renovation project to boost tenant satisfaction, only to later regret the expense when it fails to attract new leases. Similarly, business owners leasing commercial spaces often make decisions driven by fear, fear of losing a prime location or being outpaced by competitors, leading them to lock into costly, long-term leases.

Joy and passion can also drive success in commercial real estate. A landlord who takes pride in their properties might go above and beyond to ensure tenant satisfaction, creating a reputation that attracts long-term clients. Property professionals who genuinely love their work often build stronger relationships with clients, fostering trust and loyalty. However, passion can sometimes lead to overinvestment, such as upgrading a property beyond what the market demands, resulting in diminished returns.

The darker side of emotional decisions in real estate often revolves around fear and regret. Buyers, whether residential or commercial, may feel pressured to make quick decisions in competitive markets, fearing they'll miss out if they hesitate.

This fear of loss, often amplified by external factors like bidding wars or aggressive marketing, can lead to overpayment or regrettable purchases.

Sellers, too, can experience regret, especially if they undervalue their property or sell too quickly without exploring better offers.

For banks and valuators, emotional decisions often come into play during appraisals or loan approvals. A valuator might subconsciously overvalue a property because they were impressed by its aesthetics or the confidence of the property manager presenting it. Banks, on the other hand, might approve a loan based on the perceived success of a commercial property, only to face challenges when the property fails to meet projections. Even in these highly analytical roles, emotions can subtly influence outcomes.

The ripple effects of emotional decisions in real estate are far-reaching.

A tenant who falls in love with a rental might overstretch their budget, leading to financial strain down the line. An investor driven by excitement might acquire a property that requires more operational oversight than anticipated, creating unforeseen stress. In both residential and commercial contexts, emotions can amplify the highs and deepen the lows, making it critical for all stakeholders to balance passion with pragmatism.

For property professionals, understanding the emotional drivers behind client decisions is a powerful tool.

A buyer might hesitate not because of the property's flaws but because they fear making the wrong choice. A seller might resist lowering their price because of the emotional significance they attach to the property.

By recognising and addressing these emotions, professionals can guide clients toward decisions that align with both their hearts and their wallets.

Chapter Conclusion and Call to Action

Emotional decisions are an undeniable part of real estate, shaping outcomes for landlords, buyers, sellers, tenants, property managers, investors, banks, and valuators alike. The key to navigating this emotional landscape is awareness, acknowledging the role emotions play while striving to balance them with logic.

The next time you face a real estate decision, ask yourself:

"Am I letting my emotions lead, and if so, how can I ensure they're guiding me in the right direction?"

By embracing this balance, you can turn emotions from a liability into an asset, making smarter, more fulfilling choices in both residential and commercial real estate.

READERS NOTES

CHAPTER 3: Cognitive Dissonance in Real Estate

Every real estate decision comes with a battle of thoughts. Whether you're a buyer, seller, landlord, tenant, investor, or professional, the choices in real estate are rarely straightforward. Conflicting priorities often pull people in different directions, creating a psychological tension known as cognitive dissonance.

This happens when our thoughts and actions are at odds, forcing us to reconcile these contradictions to move forward. In real estate, these internal conflicts often shape the decisions we make.

Take a tenant deciding between a spacious, modern apartment that's slightly over budget and a smaller, more affordable unit. Their desire for comfort conflicts with their need for financial prudence, and reconciling this can be stressful. Similarly, a commercial tenant may face a similar dilemma when considering whether to lease a large industrial space with room for growth or a smaller space that better suits their current needs.

Real Estate decisions often involve weighing short-term costs against long-term goals, and the resolution isn't always logical.

Sellers experience cognitive dissonance too, particularly when pricing their properties. A residential seller might feel their home is worth more due to its sentimental value, while market realities suggest otherwise. This conflict between emotional attachment and financial necessity can delay decisions or lead to pricing that alienates buyers. On the commercial side, a property developer might struggle with whether to lower the asking price on a vacant office building to attract tenants or hold firm, hoping to secure a higher-paying lease. These decisions aren't just financial, they're deeply tied to pride and perception.

For buyers, cognitive dissonance is practically built into the process.

Residential buyers often wrestle with whether to stretch their budget for a dream home or settle for something more practical. They might love the charm of a green property but worry about the additional costs of sustainability upgrades. In the commercial world, investors face similar challenges. Should they prioritise long-term leases that offer stability or shorter leases with the potential for higher returns? Every decision comes with trade-offs, and the psychological weight of these trade-offs is significant.

Landlords and property managers aren't immune to cognitive dissonance either.

A landlord might debate whether to require a large deposit to secure financial safety or opt for a smaller deposit to attract more tenants quickly. A property manager overseeing a mixed-use development might face tension between allocating more resources to high-visibility commercial tenants versus smaller, long-term residential tenants. Balancing these competing interests requires constant evaluation and compromises that don't always feel entirely satisfying.

Building contractors, interior designers, and architects often experience cognitive dissonance when working on projects that balance client demands with practical constraints. A contractor might want to deliver a project quickly to stay within budget, but the quality-focused vision of the architect could slow things down. Similarly, interior designers may face conflicting client requests, like creating a luxurious space on a modest budget. These professionals must find a middle ground that satisfies everyone without sacrificing their own standards.

Banks and evaluators also encounter cognitive dissonance during their assessments.

A bank may feel torn between approving a mortgage for a promising first-time buyer who lacks surety and denying the application due to risk concerns. Evaluators might struggle to reconcile a property's aesthetic appeal with its structural realities, especially when those two factors lead to different conclusions about its value. The balance between cautious decision-making and opportunity-seizing creates a constant tension.

Investors and property developers regularly navigate dissonance in their decisions, especially when pursuing new projects. Should they focus on green buildings that align with sustainability goals, or should they prioritise cost-efficiency to maximise returns? Town planners and quantity surveyors face similar conflicts. A town planner might feel torn between approving a high-density development that boosts the local economy and preserving the character of a neighbourhood. A quantity surveyor, on the other hand, may need to balance delivering a project on budget with the pressure to accommodate last-minute design changes.

Reconciling tensions often requires stepping back to evaluate priorities and compromises.

Some people lean into rationalisation, convincing themselves that the decision they made was the only logical choice. Others rely on external validation from professionals, hoping that an architect, contractor, or property manager can provide clarity.

In the end, finding balance is about aligning actions with goals, even if the journey to get there is emotionally taxing.

Chapter Conclusion and Call to Action

Cognitive dissonance is an unavoidable part of real estate, touching everyone from tenants and buyers to landlords, architects, and banks. The key to navigating it is awareness. Recognising when conflicting thoughts arise can help you take a step back, weigh your priorities, and make decisions that align with both your practical needs and emotional goals.

The next time you feel pulled in different directions, ask yourself:

"What matters most here, and how can I reconcile the rest?"

By addressing this tension head-on, you can transform conflict into clarity and make confident, balanced choices in residential and commercial real estate.

READERS NOTES

29

CHAPTER 4: Anchoring Bias in Real Estate

Every decision we make starts with a first impression, and in real estate, that impression often comes in the form of a number.

This psychological phenomenon, known as anchoring bias, is when people rely too heavily on the first piece of information they receive, the "anchor", to make decisions. Whether it's the initial asking price of a property, the quoted rental rate, or a suggested valuation, this anchor shapes perceptions of value and sets expectations for buyers, tenants, sellers, and even professionals like real estate agents and valuators.

For residential buyers, anchoring bias often takes root the moment they see a property's price tag. A home listed at five million rand immediately frames the buyer's perception of what it's worth, even if comparable homes in the area sell for less. The buyer might justify this price based on the property's charm or a well-maintained garden, without digging deeper into market data. Similarly, tenants searching for a rental property can be influenced by the initial rental rate, which sets their expectations for what they'll find within their budget. Even if a higher-priced apartment offers better long-term value, they may disregard it simply because the anchor was too high.

Sellers also experience anchoring bias, though from the opposite perspective. A seller who believes their property is worth a certain amount, perhaps based on a neighbour's recent sale or their own emotional attachment, will anchor to that number, often ignoring market feedback. This is particularly common in residential real estate, where sentimentality plays a large role. On the commercial side, a seller might anchor to a previous appraisal or an overly optimistic projection from an asset manager, leading to unrealistic pricing that deters potential investors.

In commercial real estate, anchoring bias can have significant implications for asset managers, property managers, and investors. When an office building is listed at a high price, investors may find themselves negotiating from that point, even if the true market value is lower. For tenants, the anchor might come in the form of quoted rental rates for prime office spaces, setting their expectations for what's "reasonable." Property managers, in turn, may struggle to align tenant expectations with market realities, especially if the anchor creates a perception of overpriced properties.

Real estate agents and valuators often find themselves navigating the effects of anchoring bias during negotiations.

An agent presenting a property must be mindful of the initial price they suggest, as it not only sets the tone for buyer or tenant expectations but also influences the seller's willingness to negotiate. A valuator, tasked with providing an objective assessment, might inadvertently reinforce an anchor if their valuation aligns too closely with the seller's expectations rather than actual market conditions. Setting the right anchor requires a delicate balance between strategy and reality.

Interior designers can also play a surprising role in anchoring bias. The visual presentation of a property often creates a perceived value that reinforces the anchor. A beautifully staged home or a well-designed commercial space can make a higher asking price feel justified, even if the property's structural or location-based drawbacks should lower its value.

Conversely, an unstaged or poorly presented property may fail to command its true worth, simply because the anchor was set too low.

Buyers' associations and tenant advocates are increasingly aware of how anchoring bias can affect their members. For example, tenants may agree to rental rates that are higher than market norms simply because they were anchored to the landlord's initial offer. Associations often recommend that tenants and buyers conduct independent research to counteract the influence of anchoring, ensuring they're not overpaying based on an arbitrary starting point.

The key to overcoming anchoring bias lies in recognising its presence and questioning the initial anchor.

Buyers and tenants should compare multiple properties to recalibrate their expectations, while sellers and property managers need to ground their pricing strategies in market data rather than subjective impressions. For real estate agents, setting a competitive anchor that attracts interest without undervaluing the property is both an art and a science. Valuators, too, must strive to remain impartial, ensuring their assessments reflect true value rather than the psychological weight of an anchor.

Ultimately, anchoring bias is a double-edged sword.

When used strategically, it can create favourable perceptions that drive negotiations and secure deals. However, when relied upon too heavily, it can distort expectations, prolong negotiations, and even lead to missed opportunities.

Understanding this bias and its influence is essential for all real estate stakeholders, from individual buyers and sellers to large organisations and professionals shaping the market.

Chapter Conclusion and Call to Action

Anchoring bias is an invisible force that shapes value perception and expectations across residential and commercial real estate.

Recognising when you're being influenced by an anchor, and learning to question its validity, can lead to smarter decisions and more successful outcomes.

Whether you're a buyer, seller, tenant, property manager, investor, or agent, ask yourself:

"Am I relying too heavily on the first number I heard, or am I looking at the bigger picture?"

By being aware of anchoring bias and using it strategically, you can navigate the real estate market with confidence and clarity. Let's anchor to success, not assumptions.

READERS NOTES

CHAPTER 5: Framing Effect in Real Estate

Framing is all about perspective. It's not just what you say, but how you say it that matters. In real estate, framing refers to the way information is presented, whether through marketing, descriptions, or even visual cues, and how that influences decisions.

A single word, a carefully crafted narrative, or a well-timed piece of advice can make a property feel more valuable, desirable, or unique. For capital market professionals, investors, married couples, singles, and families alike, understanding framing can be the difference between a successful transaction and a missed opportunity.

For families looking to buy a home, framing often starts with how the property is described. A house advertised as "perfect for raising children" creates a vision of safety, growth, and legacy, even if it's not the biggest or newest on the market.

On the other hand, the same home could be framed as a "cozy retreat" to attract retirees or a "smart investment opportunity" for young professionals.

The core features of real estate remain unchanged, but the way it's marketed influences how each group sees its potential.

For investors and capital market professionals, framing plays a significant role in how opportunities are evaluated. A commercial property described as "a thriving retail hub" might stand out more than one simply listed as "centrally located."

The narrative matters because it shapes how potential buyers or tenants imagine their returns. Even subtle phrases like "future-ready office space" or "located in an emerging growth area" can create excitement about long-term potential, even if the immediate numbers don't fully support it.

Married couples often face framing effects when balancing emotional and financial priorities. A listing might highlight a home's "open floor plan, perfect for entertaining," which appeals to the couple's social aspirations, even if the property is slightly over budget.

Similarly, a house with "low-maintenance landscaping" might appeal to busy families looking to save time, even if they had originally hoped for a larger yard.

Emotional triggers, embedded in the narrative, can guide decisions in ways that feel logical in the moment but may not align with long-term goals.

In commercial real estate, framing is often tied to marketing strategies. A family-owned building might be framed as a "legacy property," appealing to investors who value long-term stability and community ties.

For single tenants or young professionals, the same building could be marketed as a "vibrant, dynamic workspace," catering to their sense of ambition and modernity. These carefully crafted narratives allow property managers to position their spaces for maximum appeal across different audiences.

Families and legacy investors are also deeply influenced by framing when planning for the future. A family might choose a property described as "ideal for multi-generational living," envisioning a home that can accommodate aging parents or growing children.

Meanwhile, an investor considering a mixed-use development may be drawn to the promise of "sustainable growth" and "community impact," even if those features come with higher upfront costs.

Framing speaks to values, aspirations, and emotions, making the decision feel personal and purposeful.

Singles, too, are affected by framing in unique ways. A single buyer might be drawn to a condominium marketed as "a stylish sanctuary in the heart of the city," valuing the lifestyle it represents.

On the commercial side, a single entrepreneur might see potential in a "versatile retail space" that fits their vision for a new business. In both cases, framing creates a connection that extends beyond the practical aspects of the property and into the realm of possibilities.

Even the presentation of pricing can be influenced by framing. A residential property listed at "under three million" might feel like a bargain, even if it's priced at 2.99 million.

Similarly, a commercial lease described as "competitive for the area" shifts the focus from cost to perceived value. These small yet powerful details demonstrate how framing can persuade and influence decisions without altering the underlying facts.

For capital market professionals and investors, framing is a tool that works both ways. It can attract clients and tenants while also shaping internal evaluations.

A seasoned investor might still feel the pull of a "high-demand property in a thriving market," even if their instincts tell them to dig deeper into the numbers. Recognising framing for what it is, a marketing strategy, helps professionals navigate these influences and stay grounded in data.

Chapter Conclusion and Call to Action

Framing effects are everywhere in real estate, influencing families, singles, investors, and capital market professionals alike.

Whether it's the way a home is described or the promise of growth tied to a commercial property, framing shapes perceptions and decisions.

The next time you're evaluating a property or opportunity, ask yourself:

"Am I being influenced by the narrative, or am I seeing the facts clearly?"

By recognising the power of framing, you can make more informed, balanced decisions that align with your goals and values. Let's take control of the frame and own the decisions we make.

READERS NOTES

CHAPTER 6: Trust Building in Real Estate

Trust is the foundation of every successful real estate transaction.

Whether you're a landlord leasing a property, a buyer making a life-changing purchase, or a lawyer representing a client in negotiations, trust underpins the confidence needed to move forward.

Trust is the intangible yet essential element that fosters connections, ensures integrity, and ultimately leads to success in both residential and commercial real estate.

For landlords and tenants, trust often begins with the first interaction. A landlord who presents a well-maintained property and clear terms builds confidence with prospective tenants.

Tenants, in turn, must trust that the landlord will address maintenance issues promptly and uphold their end of the agreement. In commercial real estate, this dynamic is amplified. A developer offering office spaces to corporate clients must ensure that every aspect, from the lease terms to building quality, inspires trust. Without it, negotiations stall, and opportunities are lost.

Buyers and sellers, whether in residential or commercial transactions, rely heavily on trust to bridge the gap between interests.

A residential buyer must trust that the seller is being transparent about the property's condition, while the seller needs to feel confident that the buyer is serious and financially capable. In commercial deals, where stakes are often higher, trust becomes even more critical.

An investor considering a mixed-use development or retail space must trust not only the seller but also the data and projections being presented. Without that trust, hesitation creeps in, derailing progress.

Agents and legal professionals play a pivotal role in building trust between parties.

Real estate agents are often the first point of contact, and their ability to communicate clearly, act ethically, and advocate for their clients sets the tone for the entire transaction.

A trustworthy agent makes both buyers and sellers feel "right at home," knowing their interests are being protected. Similarly, attorneys and solicitors must demonstrate integrity and thoroughness, ensuring that contracts are fair and all legal aspects are covered. A single misstep can erode trust, making future collaboration difficult.

For real estate developers and financiers, trust is the linchpin of long-term success.

A developer pitching a new project to investors must establish credibility by delivering clear plans, realistic timelines, and transparent financials. Financiers, whether banks or private lenders, need to trust that the project will generate returns and that their capital is secure. In residential real estate, trust between developers and buyers is equally important.

Off-plan purchases, for example, require buyers to trust that the developer will deliver on promises, which can be daunting without a solid reputation.

Real estate investors often face the challenge of evaluating trustworthiness in potential partners or opportunities.

A landlord offering a multi-family property for sale might present attractive figures, but the investor must trust that these projections are based on reality, not inflated optimism.

Similarly, an attorney or legal counsel reviewing the deal must ensure that all details are accurate, fostering confidence for the client to proceed.

In real estate dynamics, trust can be fragile.

A seller who withholds information about structural issues risks not only losing the sale but also damaging their reputation. Conversely, a buyer who fails to meet deadlines or negotiate in good faith may find it hard to secure deals in the future.

This delicate balance of trust is what keeps the real estate market functioning smoothly, whether for single-family homes or high-rise office spaces.

Legal professionals often act as the glue that holds transactions together, ensuring that trust is not breached. A solicitor drafting a lease agreement for a commercial tenant must make sure both parties feel protected, while an attorney overseeing a residential sale ensures that all disclosures are made.

This attention to detail builds confidence, allowing parties to move forward without fear of hidden risks.

In the fast-paced world of real estate, trust also extends to the broader relationships that underpin the industry. A financier trusting a developer to deliver a profitable project, a landlord trusting a property manager to oversee tenants effectively, or even a buyer trusting a home inspector's evaluation, each of these scenarios highlights the critical role trust plays in every aspect of the field.

Without trust, even the most promising opportunities can fall apart.

(PS: If you want to take a deeper dive into trust, read my book *Economics of Banking and Money: Insight into Power, Trust, and Change*.)

Chapter Conclusion and Call to Action

Trust is the currency of real estate, enabling landlords, buyers, sellers, developers, investors, attorneys, and financiers to collaborate effectively and achieve success. Building and maintaining trust requires integrity, clear communication, and a commitment to transparency at every stage of a transaction.

The next time you enter a real estate deal, ask yourself:

"Am I fostering trust with every interaction?"

By focusing on trust, you'll not only strengthen connections but also create a foundation for long-term success. Let's build trust, and the deals will follow.

READERS NOTES

CHAPTER 7: Scarcity Mindset in Real Estate

In real estate, scarcity can feel like a ticking clock. Whether you're a buyer, seller, landlord, tenant, developer, or investor, the perception of limited availability can create a powerful sense of urgency.

This scarcity mindset drives demand, intensifies competition, and shapes decisions in ways that are often more emotional than logical. It's not just about the property, it's about the fear of missing out on what seems like a rare opportunity.

For residential buyers, scarcity often appears in the form of competitive bidding. Imagine walking into an open house and finding it packed with other potential buyers. Suddenly, that house feels even more desirable, not because it changed overnight, but because the demand creates a sense of urgency. Sellers know this too and often use scarcity as a strategy, setting tight offer deadlines or hinting at other interested parties.

Scarcity creates a race, and in that race, buyers and tenants may find themselves overbidding or compromising on their ideal terms.

For property developers, scarcity is both a tool and a challenge. Developers often create a sense of exclusivity by limiting the availability of units in a residential complex or commercial building. By marketing phrases like "only two units left" or "limited-time pricing," they tap into the desire to act quickly before the opportunity slips away. On the other hand, developers also face scarcity themselves, scarcity of prime land, building materials, or financing, which can lead to increased competition among peers and higher project costs.

In commercial real estate, the scarcity mindset is equally prevalent. Tenants looking for office space in a high-demand area might feel pressured to sign a lease quickly, fearing that waiting could result in losing out. Landlords, aware of this, often use scarcity as leverage, framing their property as a rare gem in a crowded market. Investors, too, are influenced by scarcity, especially when a sought-after retail space or industrial warehouse becomes available.

The perception that "if you don't act now, someone else will" can push decisions faster than thorough evaluations might suggest.

Financiers and lenders are not immune to the scarcity mindset either. A bank evaluating a loan application for a commercial property might prioritise it if the developer presents the project as a rare opportunity in a booming area.

Similarly, investors seeking to back new developments often face stiff competition, especially when the project promises high returns. The desire to secure these opportunities can lead to rushed decisions, bypassing deeper due diligence in favour of speed.

For landlords and tenants, scarcity often shapes lease negotiations. A landlord with a desirable property may set higher rents or stricter terms, knowing that tenants will feel compelled to accept rather than risk losing the space.

Tenants, especially in highly competitive markets, might agree to leases they'd normally avoid, simply because the scarcity mindset convinces them there are no better options.

This dynamic plays out in real estate rentals, where tenants may scramble to secure a lease, fearing they'll be left without a property if they hesitate.

The scarcity mindset doesn't just impact individuals, it also shapes entire market trends.

A neighbourhood with a limited number of available homes can see property values skyrocket, driven by the perception of exclusivity. In commercial real estate, the presence of a few high-demand properties can elevate the perceived value of the surrounding area, creating ripple effects that influence developers, investors, and even tenants.

Scarcity, whether real or manufactured, has a way of amplifying competition and intensifying desire.

Property professionals, from agents to developers, often rely on the scarcity mindset as part of their strategy. By framing a property as a limited opportunity, they appeal to the emotional side of decision-making. Buyers and tenants may act faster and with fewer reservations when they feel time is running out.

At the same time, professionals must balance this approach with integrity, overusing scarcity as a tactic can backfire, leading to mistrust or unrealistic expectations.

Ultimately, the scarcity mindset can be both a motivator and a trap.

While it drives action and creates opportunities, it can also cloud judgment and lead to rushed decisions.

Recognising when scarcity is being used as a tool, and separating genuine urgency from artificial pressure, is essential for making sound real estate choices, whether you're buying your first home, leasing a commercial space, or investing in a major development.

Chapter Conclusion and Call to Action

The scarcity mindset is a powerful force in real estate, influencing buyers, sellers, tenants, landlords, developers, and financiers alike. By creating urgency and intensifying competition, it shapes decisions and drives markets.

The next time you find yourself in a competitive situation, ask:

"Am I acting on facts, or am I reacting to scarcity?"

Understanding this mindset can help you navigate the pressure with clarity, making choices that align with your goals rather than the ticking clock. Let's approach scarcity wisely, turning urgency into opportunity.

READERS NOTES

CHAPTER 8: Social Proof in Real Estate

Social proof plays a critical role in how people make decisions in real estate. It's about observing others' actions and using that as a guide, especially when faced with uncertainty.

Whether it's a buyer choosing a popular neighborhood or a landlord setting rents based on market demand, the influence of community trends is undeniable. Let's dive into how this concept impacts buyers, sellers, landlords, tenants, banks, and property professionals.

For buyers, location often sets the tone. Neighborhoods with good reputations, like family-friendly communities or areas with strong schools, quickly become hotspots. This isn't limited to residential buyers; commercial investors also look at areas where businesses are thriving, confident that popularity equals stability. Buyers feel validated when others have made similar choices, which reinforces the perception of value and security.

Beyond location, the property type itself can also be shaped by trends.

For instance, in residential real estate, energy-efficient homes have become increasingly popular due to societal emphasis on sustainability. Commercial buyers, similarly, look for properties with modern amenities or flexible workspaces as influenced by current market preferences.

Sellers often use social proof to their advantage. Open houses filled with visitors send a message that the property is in high demand. Highlighting nearby recent sales or booming trends can also justify a higher price point. In commercial real estate, showcasing a tenant roster with reputable businesses signals an appealing and trustworthy investment. Sellers know that by emphasizing these elements, they can tap into buyers' need for validation. A property with a strong story of desirability often attracts multiple offers, further enhancing its appeal. They also rely on market timing, choosing moments when public interest in certain areas or types of property is at its peak, to ensure maximum returns.

Landlords benefit just as much from social proof.

Residential tenants gravitate toward buildings where they see stability, like happy neighbors or consistent demand. Commercial landlords, on the other hand, know the value of securing an anchor tenant, a well-known business that attracts others to lease in the same location. A property that looks popular is easier to rent out at competitive rates. Additionally, online reviews and word-of-mouth recommendations have become critical in shaping prospective tenants' perceptions. Positive reviews often translate to higher occupancy rates, while negative feedback can deter even the most eager renters. Landlords who actively manage their reputation can leverage social proof to maintain strong demand.

Tenants, too, rely on social proof. For residential renters, knowing others are moving into a complex often reassures them about their choice. Commercial tenants follow a similar logic; they'll often consider the reputation of nearby businesses before signing a lease.

This clustering of reputable brands enhances the value of the entire location, benefiting everyone involved.

A coffee shop might be more inclined to lease a space if it's next to a gym or co-working space, as these attract consistent foot traffic. Similarly, residential tenants prefer buildings with well-established communities, often checking social media or local forums to gauge the vibe of the area before committing.

Banks and financiers are not immune to the pull of social proof. They tend to approve loans for projects in areas with rising popularity and strong development trends. This makes it easier for developers and investors to secure funding in places where others have already seen success. Social proof reduces perceived risk, making the bank more confident in its decisions. For instance, a lender may be more inclined to finance a shopping center if several established brands have already committed to leases. On the other hand, areas perceived as losing favor may struggle to attract financing, even if individual projects show promise. Banks use market trends as a safety net, trusting that community momentum will safeguard their investments.

Property professionals understand this concept intimately. Agents and brokers often use market trends and success stories to instill confidence in their clients.

Developers also rely on pre-sales and media buzz to demonstrate demand. Highlighting social proof is one of the most effective ways to reassure buyers and sellers about their decisions. For example, an agent might share data showing that similar properties in the area have been selling quickly, prompting buyers to act fast. Developers, meanwhile, use promotional campaigns to highlight early sales, creating a sense of urgency and validation for potential buyers. By capitalizing on social proof, professionals can create a competitive edge for their clients.

Social proof is a cornerstone of real estate decision-making.

Whether you're navigating residential or commercial markets, it's a force that shapes trends, influences value, and validates choices. For a deeper exploration of this topic and its economic implications, I encourage you to read my book, *Real Estate Economics, Property Market Principles and Practices*. It offers practical insights into how social proof and other dynamics drive the market.

Chapter Conclusion and Call to Action

Social proof is a compelling force, shaping decisions across all facets of real estate. From buyers and sellers to landlords, tenants, and banks, it influences perceptions and creates trends.

The next time you're faced with a property decision, ask yourself:

"Am I making this choice based on thoughtful research, or am I simply following the crowd?"

By understanding the mechanics of social proof, you can make choices that align with your goals.

READERS NOTES

CHAPTER 9: Heuristic Thinking in Real Estate

Heuristic thinking is a concept rooted in mental shortcuts. It is the quick, intuitive judgments we make to simplify complex decisions. In real estate, where choices can often feel overwhelming, these shortcuts help buyers, sellers, landlords, tenants, property managers, and investors act more efficiently.

However, while heuristics can save time, they also come with risks, as they can lead to oversights or snap judgments. Understanding this type of thinking is crucial to navigating the complexities of real estate with greater clarity and confidence.

For buyers, heuristics often manifest as gut feelings. A residential buyer might walk into a house and immediately feel it's perfect, the lighting, the layout, and even the neighborhood all seem to check the boxes. Similarly, a commercial buyer might choose a property in a bustling area, assuming the location guarantees success.

While these instincts can be useful, relying solely on them can lead to mistakes.

That dream home might have hidden structural issues, and that seemingly ideal commercial space might face logistical challenges. Balancing intuition with thorough research helps buyers make sounder decisions.

Sellers also rely on heuristic thinking, especially when determining how to price their properties. A residential seller might base their price on what a neighbor's home sold for, assuming all homes in the area are comparable. On the commercial side, a seller might highlight prestigious tenants in the vicinity to justify a higher price.

While these mental shortcuts make pricing decisions easier, they can lead to inaccuracies.

Landlords use heuristics frequently when screening tenants. A residential landlord might approve a tenant who appears polite and professional, assuming those traits ensure reliability, without conducting a full background check. In commercial leasing, landlords might prioritize securing a well-known tenant, believing their presence will elevate the property's reputation.

While these shortcuts can yield positive outcomes, they also come with risks.

Overlooking important details, such as a tenant's financial stability or maintenance responsibilities, can create long-term problems.

Tenants, both residential and commercial, are influenced by heuristic thinking. A residential tenant might choose an apartment because it's close to work, ignoring other factors like building management or neighborhood safety. Similarly, a commercial tenant might select a space based on foot traffic alone, assuming it will automatically lead to business success. While these judgments make decision-making faster, they can lead to regrets if tenants fail to consider the bigger picture.

Property professionals, including agents and managers, often use heuristics to streamline their processes.

An agent might focus on showing properties similar to those recently sold, assuming these are what buyers are looking for. A property manager might repeatedly hire the same contractors based on past experiences, without exploring potentially better options. While these shortcuts save time, they can limit opportunities for growth or improvement if not balanced with broader evaluation.

Investors frequently rely on heuristic thinking, especially in fast-paced markets. A residential investor might buy a fixer-upper in a developing area based on a hunch that property values will rise. A commercial investor might commit to a project because it aligns with market trends, trusting their instincts about demand.

While intuition plays a vital role in spotting opportunities, relying on it alone can lead to costly mistakes. Combining gut feelings with detailed analysis ensures better outcomes.

Understanding heuristic thinking doesn't mean abandoning mental shortcuts altogether. Instead, it's about recognizing when these shortcuts are helpful and when they might lead to oversight. By pausing to reflect on how and why decisions are made, everyone involved in real estate can strike a balance between efficiency and thoroughness. This approach leads to more confident and informed decision-making, no matter the role.

Chapter Conclusion and Call to Action

Heuristic thinking simplifies decision-making in real estate, helping buyers, sellers, landlords, tenants, and investors act quickly. However, these shortcuts can sometimes lead to errors when used carelessly.

The next time you face a property decision, ask yourself:

"Am I relying too heavily on intuition, or have I considered all the relevant facts?"

By understanding and balancing heuristic thinking with deliberate research, you can make decisions that align with your goals.

For more insights on great decision-making in real estate, explore my book, *Raising Money for Real Estate Investment*. It is a practical guide to secure funding for real estate projects, and emphasizes effective thinking and deal-making strategies.

READERS NOTES

CHAPTER 10: Hedonic Adaptation in Real Estate

Hedonic adaptation is a fascinating concept. It's the idea that people quickly adjust to changes in their living conditions, whether those changes are positive or negative.

In real estate, this can play a powerful role in shaping how buyers, tenants, and even property owners feel about their decisions over time. That initial burst of joy from moving into a new home or securing a prime commercial space often fades as people adapt to their new surroundings.

Understanding this cycle can help us make better decisions and plan for lasting satisfaction in property choices.

For residential buyers, hedonic adaptation often starts with the excitement of buying a new home. Everything feels fresh and exciting during the first few months, from the updated kitchen to the cozy backyard. But as time goes on, that novelty begins to wear off. A home that once felt like a dream can start to feel ordinary, or even less appealing, as small inconveniences become more noticeable. This is why some homeowners constantly look for bigger spaces, better neighborhoods, or more luxurious features, believing these changes will bring lasting happiness. The cycle of adaptation often fuels a desire for more, making it important to balance dreams with practical needs.

In commercial real estate, hedonic adaptation can influence business owners and tenants alike. A new office space or retail location might feel perfect initially, offering a boost in morale or foot traffic. Over time, though, the same space might feel limiting or outdated as the excitement wears off. Business owners might begin to notice issues they initially overlooked, such as layout inefficiencies or maintenance challenges. This can lead to a restlessness that pushes tenants to seek out newer or more appealing locations.

Understanding this tendency helps property managers and landlords anticipate their clients' changing needs and adapt their offerings to retain long-term tenants.

Landlords, both residential and commercial, also experience hedonic adaptation. A landlord might feel immense pride when their property is fully occupied or generates consistent income. But as time passes, they may start to focus on challenges like tenant turnover, maintenance demands, or market fluctuations. This shift in perspective often leads landlords to invest in renovations or updates, aiming to reignite the satisfaction they initially felt. While these upgrades can add value, it's important to consider whether they align with tenant preferences and market trends, rather than just the landlord's desire for change.

Tenants, too, are deeply affected by hedonic adaptation. A residential tenant might initially fall in love with an apartment for its modern design or great location. But after living there for a while, they might begin to notice flaws. Perhaps the building is noisier than expected, or the commute isn't as convenient as it seemed. Similarly, a commercial tenant might be thrilled with a high-visibility retail space, only to feel dissatisfied later if customer traffic doesn't meet their expectations.

This natural adjustment process often prompts tenants to move or renegotiate leases, highlighting the importance of addressing their evolving needs.

Agents often work with clients who are chasing the next big thing, whether it's a more luxurious home or a better investment property. By helping clients understand the cycle of adaptation, professionals can guide them toward choices that balance emotional satisfaction with long-term practicality.

Managers, on the other hand, can use this understanding to enhance tenant retention by addressing concerns early and consistently updating properties to meet modern standards.

Property professionals, including agents and managers, play a key role in navigating hedonic adaptation.

For investors, hedonic adaptation can shape both expectations and decisions. A residential investor might initially feel great about acquiring a promising rental property, but over time, they might become restless and look for larger or more lucrative investments.

Commercial investors often face a similar cycle, starting with high enthusiasm for a new development only to feel dissatisfied when market conditions shift or the initial excitement fades.

Recognizing this tendency can help investors maintain perspective and focus on long-term value rather than short-term gratification.

Hedonic adaptation doesn't mean people can't find lasting satisfaction in real estate. Instead, it highlights the importance of awareness and intentionality.

By understanding how quickly people adjust to changes, we can make choices that foster comfort and contentment over the long term, whether we're buying, renting, or managing properties.

Chapter Conclusion and Call to Action

Hedonic adaptation is a natural part of life, influencing how we perceive and value our properties over time.

From buyers and tenants to landlords and investors, this cycle of adjustment shapes satisfaction and drives change in real estate.

The next time you consider a property decision, ask yourself:

"Am I seeking real comfort and value, or am I chasing the fleeting excitement of something new?"

By recognising this dynamic, you can make choices that align with both your current needs and future goals.

READERS NOTES

CHAPTER 11: Loss Aversion in Real Estate

Loss aversion is a powerful force in real estate. People often fear losing money or opportunities more than they value the excitement of gains. This fear shapes decisions for buyers, sellers, landlords, developers, and financiers, often causing hesitation or overly cautious behavior.

By understanding how loss aversion influences behavior, we can learn to navigate real estate with more clarity and confidence.

For buyers, loss aversion often appears as a reluctance to overpay. A residential buyer might hesitate to bid higher in a competitive market, fearing they'll lose money if the market dips later. Commercial buyers, on the other hand, may delay purchasing a property, worrying that they're buying at the peak of the market cycle. While this caution can protect against losses, it can also lead to missed opportunities when great properties are passed up due to fear.

The key in real estate is balancing caution with informed decision-making.

Sellers also experience loss aversion, particularly when pricing their properties. A residential seller might set an asking price based on an emotional attachment to what they believe their home is worth, fearing they'll lose money if they accept less. In commercial real estate, sellers may hold out for higher offers, worried about leaving money on the table, even when the market suggests a quicker sale would be wiser.

Fear of loss can sometimes backfire, leading to properties sitting on the market for too long and ultimately selling for less than anticipated.

Landlords face their own struggles with loss aversion. A residential landlord might fear losing good tenants by raising rents, even when the market supports an increase. On the flip side, they might hesitate to invest in property improvements, worrying the costs won't translate into higher rental income. Commercial landlords often face similar dilemmas. They may avoid taking risks on new tenants, fearing potential defaults, or resist renegotiating lease terms even when doing so could benefit both parties.

Decisions, driven by fear, can limit growth and reduce long-term profitability.

Loss aversion also affects developers, particularly when undertaking large projects. Residential developers might delay breaking ground on new housing developments, concerned about market volatility or rising construction costs. Similarly, commercial developers may hesitate to invest in innovative projects, fearing they won't recoup their expenses if demand doesn't materialize as expected.

While caution is necessary, excessive fear of loss can stifle creativity and innovation, preventing you from seizing lucrative opportunities.

Financiers and bankers are not immune to the effects of loss aversion. Lenders often adopt conservative approaches, fearing defaults and financial losses. For residential properties, a bank might hesitate to approve a loan for a first-time buyer with a less-than-perfect credit history, even when market trends suggest low risk. In commercial real estate, banks may restrict lending for speculative projects, worried about market downturns or oversupply.

While risk management is essential, overly cautious financing can limit growth and innovation in the industry.

Loss aversion can also lead to counterproductive behavior. Buyers might back out of deals due to minor concerns, only to regret it later. Sellers might reject reasonable offers, only to find themselves reducing prices months down the line. Landlords might avoid necessary updates, leading to tenant dissatisfaction and higher turnover. Developers and financiers, too, may find themselves missing out on prime opportunities due to fear of short-term losses.

Recognizing these patterns and addressing them thoughtfully is crucial for success in real estate.

Understanding loss aversion doesn't mean ignoring risks. Instead, it's about recognizing when fear is clouding judgment and balancing it with rational decision-making. Real estate, after all, is as much about managing emotions as it is about managing assets.

By staying focused on long-term goals and remaining adaptable, we can make decisions that lead to lasting success.

Chapter Conclusion and Call to Action

Loss aversion drives many decisions in real estate, shaping how buyers, sellers, landlords, developers, and financiers approach opportunities.

While caution can be valuable, excessive fear of loss often leads to missed chances and stagnation.

The next time you face a property decision, ask yourself:

"Am I holding back out of fear, or am I making a calculated choice?"

By understanding loss aversion, you can navigate real estate decisions with confidence and clarity.

READERS NOTES

CHAPTER 12: Endowment Effect in Real Estate

The endowment effect is a psychological phenomenon where people place a higher value on things they own simply because they own them. In real estate, this effect often shows up when sellers overestimate the worth of their properties or when landlords feel their investments are more valuable than the market suggests.

Buyers, tenants, and even banks are influenced by this bias, which can lead to both opportunities and challenges in residential and commercial real estate.

Understanding the endowment effect helps us approach property decisions with greater clarity and balance.

For sellers, the endowment effect is particularly strong. A homeowner might believe their house is worth far more than market appraisals because of personal memories tied to the space. That backyard where the kids played or the custom renovations they made feel invaluable, leading sellers to set unrealistic asking prices. In commercial real estate, a business owner might overvalue their property because of the years of effort and success they've poured into it. While this emotional attachment is natural, it can hinder the ability to sell at a competitive price. Recognizing the endowment effect allows sellers to approach pricing with a more objective perspective.

Landlords, too, often experience the endowment effect. A residential landlord might overvalue their rental property, insisting on higher rents because they see it as superior to other units on the market. Commercial landlords might refuse to negotiate lease terms, convinced that their property offers unmatched value. This can result in prolonged vacancies or difficulty attracting tenants.

While pride in ownership is a strength, landlords who balance their emotional connection with market realities often achieve better outcomes.

For buyers, the endowment effect can shape negotiations. Residential buyers might pay a premium for a property because they imagine how it will feel to make it their own, even if similar homes are available at lower prices. In commercial real estate, buyers may overlook more practical options in favor of properties they perceive as status symbols or future landmarks.

While the endowment effect can inspire confidence in a decision, it's essential to align emotional value with financial logic.

Tenants also encounter the endowment effect, particularly when they've occupied a property for a long time. A residential tenant might resist moving from an apartment they've grown attached to, even when a better opportunity arises. Similarly, a commercial tenant may overvalue their current lease space, believing it's essential to their business's success, despite rising costs or declining advantages.

Recognizing this bias in real estate can help make decisions that align with long-term goals rather than clinging to familiarity.

Property managers often deal with the impact of the endowment effect when mediating between landlords and tenants. A manager might need to convince a landlord to adjust their expectations or help tenants see the benefits of moving to a new property. This requires tact and a deep understanding of both market trends and human psychology. Managers who navigate these conversations effectively can create solutions that satisfy all parties involved.

Even banks and financiers are influenced by the endowment effect. A lender might overestimate the security of a property as collateral, especially if it's been a successful investment in the past. Residential mortgage providers may also lean toward properties with perceived stability, sometimes overlooking more innovative or unconventional opportunities.

Balancing emotional biases with hard data allows financial institutions to make sounder lending decisions that benefit their clients and themselves.

The endowment effect isn't inherently negative. It reflects the pride and attachment people feel toward what they've built or invested in. However, unchecked, it can lead to decisions driven more by emotion than by logic. By acknowledging this bias, everyone in the real estate world from buyers and sellers to landlords and banks can make choices that better align with their goals and the realities of the market.

Chapter Conclusion and Call to Action

The endowment effect is a powerful force in real estate, shaping how people perceive and value properties.

Whether you're buying, selling, renting, or managing, understanding this phenomenon helps you balance emotional attachment with practical decision-making.

The next time you face a property decision, ask yourself:

"Am I valuing this based on facts, or is my attachment clouding my judgment?"

For more insights on fact versus attachment, kindly consider my book, *Proven Principles of Residential Real Estate Investment*. It's a strategy guide, designed to help readers achieve long-term financial security and success.

READERS NOTES

CHAPTER 13: Status Quo Bias in Real Estate

Status quo bias explains why people often resist change in real estate. Whether it's holding onto a home that no longer fits their needs or sticking with an investment out of habit, many individuals prefer the comfort of the familiar over the uncertainty of something new.

This tendency to avoid change can be both a safety net and a barrier to growth. Understanding how status quo bias impacts decision-making is key for anyone navigating residential or commercial real estate.

For homeowners, the bias often shows up as reluctance to sell. A family may feel deeply attached to their house, even if it has become too small or too far from work. They focus on the memories they've built there and fear the disruption that comes with moving. Similarly, in commercial real estate, a business owner might resist relocating to a more suitable space, worried about losing clients or disrupting their operations.

While these feelings are natural, they can prevent people from taking steps that could improve their lives or businesses in the long run.

Landlords often face status quo bias when managing their properties. A residential landlord may hesitate to update an older building, believing tenants are content with the current state of things. On the commercial side, a landlord might keep outdated office spaces, thinking long-term tenants prefer stability over modern amenities. This resistance to change can result in lost opportunities to attract higher-paying tenants or increase property value. Landlords who recognize the value of adaptation can better position themselves in competitive markets.

Property managers frequently encounter status quo bias when mediating between landlords and tenants. A manager might find that tenants resist rent increases, even if the changes align with market trends and improved amenities. Conversely, landlords might push back against tenant requests for updates or upgrades, clinging to the idea that what worked in the past will work in the future.

Navigating these dynamics requires an understanding of the emotional resistance that underpins many real estate decisions.

Developers also feel the pull of status quo bias, particularly when investing in projects. A residential developer might hesitate to venture into newer markets, favoring areas they've worked in before. Commercial developers might stick to traditional building designs, fearing that more innovative concepts could alienate investors or tenants. While this preference for stability can mitigate risks, it may also lead to missed opportunities in emerging markets or evolving industries. Developers who push past these biases often find ways to balance familiarity with innovation.

Even financial institutions are not immune to status quo bias. Banks and lenders might prefer funding established projects over riskier, innovative developments.

For residential mortgages, they may favor traditional borrowers with predictable profiles, overlooking first-time buyers or unconventional investments.

In commercial real estate, they may back projects in proven markets rather than exploring opportunities in growing regions.

While conservative approach protects against loss, it can also limit growth in areas that require forward-thinking investments.

Status quo bias can lead to stability, but it can also create stagnation. A property owner might miss out on rising markets, a developer could overlook transformative opportunities, and tenants might stay in less-than-ideal spaces longer than necessary.

Recognizing this tendency doesn't mean abandoning stability; instead, it means balancing comfort with the courage to explore new possibilities. Real estate, after all, thrives on a mix of stability and calculated risk.

Chapter Conclusion and Call to Action

Status quo bias influences many real estate decisions, often keeping people tied to the familiar rather than embracing change. From homeowners and landlords to developers and financiers, this resistance can shape behavior in ways that limit potential growth.

The next time you face a property decision, ask yourself:

"Am I choosing stability for the right reasons, or am I letting fear of change hold me back?"

By understanding and challenging status quo bias, you can unlock new opportunities in both residential and commercial real estate.

READERS NOTES

CHAPTER 14: Sunk Cost Fallacy in Real Estate

The sunk cost fallacy is a powerful and often misunderstood concept in real estate. It describes the tendency to continue investing in a property or project simply because of the time, money, or effort already spent, even when it's clear that walking away might be the wiser choice.

In both residential and commercial real estate, this fallacy influences buyers, sellers, landlords, developers, and even real estate professionals. Understanding how sunk costs can cloud judgment is essential for making better decisions and avoiding further losses.

For homeowners, sunk cost often comes in the form of emotional attachment and prior investments. A homeowner who has spent years renovating their house may resist selling it for less than they believe it's worth, even if market conditions have changed. They focus on the money spent on improvements rather than the reality of the current market value. Similarly, in commercial real estate, a business owner might continue operating in an underperforming location because they've already poured significant funds into the space.

While it's natural to feel committed to past investments, clinging to them can prevent people from making choices that would lead to better outcomes.

Landlords frequently encounter the sunk cost fallacy when managing their properties. A residential landlord might hold onto a rental property with declining returns, believing that their initial investment will eventually pay off. On the commercial side, a landlord might hesitate to convert outdated office space into more modern configurations, focusing on the costs of past construction rather than the benefits of future upgrades. This reluctance to adapt can lead to stagnant income and missed opportunities to attract higher-paying tenants.

Recognizing when it's time to move forward is key to staying competitive in a changing market.

Property developers are particularly susceptible to sunk costs, given the scale of their investments. A residential developer might continue with a project in a slowing market, hoping to recoup expenses even when demand has shifted. In commercial developments, a project that runs over budget may push developers to keep pouring in money, fearing the reputational and financial costs of abandoning it.

While commitment is important in any venture, the sunk cost fallacy can blind developers to better alternatives, such as pivoting to a new strategy or exiting the project entirely.

Real estate professionals, including agents and managers, also experience sunk costs in the form of time and effort. An agent might continue marketing a property that has little chance of selling because of the hours already invested.

A property manager might stick with underperforming vendors or outdated practices, focusing on the resources already spent instead of the potential gains from change.

This bias often prevents professionals from re-evaluating their strategies and finding more efficient paths to success.

Even banks and financiers aren't immune to the sunk cost fallacy. A lender might continue funding a struggling development because of the significant loans already extended, rather than cutting losses and reallocating resources.

In residential lending, banks may hesitate to adjust terms for borrowers in difficulty, focusing instead on recovering what's already owed.

While financial institutions are structured to minimize risk, sunk cost bias can still lead to decisions that prolong losses rather than mitigate them.

Time is one of the most overlooked sunk costs in real estate. Developers, agents, and even tenants often fail to account for the value of the time spent on unproductive projects or properties.

A developer who delays a decision in hopes of salvaging a troubled project not only incurs financial costs but also loses valuable time that could be spent on more promising ventures. Similarly, tenants who stay in unsuitable spaces because of the effort involved in moving may miss out on opportunities that would better align with their needs.

Recognizing the value of time as a resource is essential for avoiding the sunk cost trap.

The sunk cost fallacy isn't about dismissing prior investments, it's about understanding when those investments no longer serve your goals.

In real estate, as in life, the hardest decisions often involve letting go of what no longer works.

By acknowledging sunk costs for what they are, you can focus on making choices that align with your future rather than clinging to the past.

Chapter Conclusion and Call to Action

As the second-to-last chapter in this book, the sunk cost fallacy provides an essential takeaway for those who have invested their time in reading.

Ask yourself: *"Has this book provided value? Will you continue to the final chapter, where the Book Summary tie everything together?"*

Recognising how past investments shape decisions can help you avoid unnecessary losses and focus on what truly matters. What truly matters now is reading the conclusion of this book.

The next time you face a tough property decision, ask yourself:

"Am I holding on because of what I've already invested, or because it's the best path forward?".

READERS NOTES

CHAPTER 15: Book Summary and Conclusion

This book has taken you on a journey through the intricate psychology of real estate, exploring how the human mind influences decisions in profound and often unexpected ways. Across these fourteen chapters, we've delved into key psychological principles and their impact on real estate behavior, from buyers and sellers to landlords, developers, and financiers.

We began with the concept of scarcity mindset, where the fear of missing out drives urgency in competitive property markets.

This idea connects seamlessly with social proof, showing how the actions of others shape our perceptions of value and desirability, whether in a family-friendly neighborhood or a bustling commercial hub. From there, heuristic thinking revealed how quick mental shortcuts guide many real estate decisions, often balancing efficiency with the risk of oversights.

Each chapter brought new layers of understanding, highlighting the emotional and cognitive forces at play.

Hedonic adaptation taught us how quickly we adjust to changes in our living or business environments, explaining why initial excitement about a property can fade over time. Similarly, the framing effect showed how presenting information in specific ways can sway decisions, whether in pricing negotiations or investment pitches.

Anchoring bias reminded us how easily the first piece of information we encounter can disproportionately influence our choices, such as a list price setting expectations for value.

Loss aversion struck a deep chord, illustrating why the fear of losing money or opportunities often outweighs the potential joy of gains.

This ties closely to the endowment effect, which explains why we overvalue what we own, whether it's a cherished home or a long-held investment property. Status quo bias further reinforced our tendency to stick with the familiar, even when change might lead to better outcomes.

Finally, the sunk cost fallacy reminded us of the importance of cutting losses when past investments no longer serve our goals, whether in personal time or financial resources.

Psychological principles can interweave beautifully when applied to real estate.

A buyer might simultaneously grapple with scarcity mindset, anchoring bias, and loss aversion, hesitating between acting too quickly or not quickly enough. A seller may overprice their property due to the endowment effect, compounded by framing decisions in a way that alienates potential buyers.

Landlords face similar struggles, resisting updates due to sunk costs or underestimating tenant needs because of status quo bias. For developers and financiers, these biases often manifest in high-stakes projects, where emotional attachment to past investments clouds judgment about future opportunities.

The examples throughout this book showcase the real-world implications of these psychological principles.

A residential buyer might chase a trendy neighborhood influenced by social proof, while a commercial investor might overcommit to a development due to sunk costs. Tenants, landlords, and real estate professionals alike face decisions shaped by these cognitive tendencies daily. Understanding how these principles interact helps us see the bigger picture, where psychology and property markets collide.

Not all is lost. With awareness and new skills, we can navigate these biases to make smarter decisions.

Whether you're a real estate professional managing high-stakes negotiations, a banker assessing risk, an investor evaluating opportunities, a developer planning the next project, or even a tenant choosing a home or office, these insights offer tools to align your choices with your goals.

Recognizing these patterns in ourselves and others isn't just empowering; it's transformative.

The beauty of real estate lies in its complexity. It is a blend of financial strategy, market knowledge, and deeply human emotions. This book has provided you with a framework to better understand your position, sharpen your skills, and approach decisions with clarity.

By applying what you've learned, you can embrace opportunities with confidence and move beyond the limits of bias and fear.

The journey doesn't end here. Each principle, from scarcity mindset to sunk costs, offers a chance to reflect, adapt, and grow.

The key is balance, between instinct and analysis, between emotion and logic.

As you continue your path in real estate, remember that every decision, no matter how challenging, is an opportunity to learn and improve. You now have the mental and cognitive tools to build success on a foundation of knowledge and self-awareness.

Thank you for taking the time to explore this book and embark on a journey to better understand the psychology and dynamics of real estate.

I hope the insights shared here empower you to make confident, informed decisions and inspire growth in your personal and professional pursuits. Wishing you all the best and every success as you navigate your real estate journey with clarity, resilience, and purpose.

At its core, this book reminds us that real estate is a mirror of human judgment. Every price, every offer, and every hesitation reflects how people see value, risk, and reward.

Psychology shapes not only what we buy or sell but how we interpret the market itself. By understanding these patterns, we gain insight into both people and property, learning that success in real estate begins not in the market, but in the mind.

READERS NOTES

Glossaries of Psychology and Real Estate

These glossaries clarify the key ideas in this book. The first explains the **psychological principles** that shape judgment and decision-making. The second defines **real estate terms** used in both residential and commercial contexts.

Together, they connect human behavior with market insight, the core theme of this work.

My wish is that you not only learn these words but use them in your day, your thinking, and your strategy as you build confidence and mastery in real estate.

Glossary of Psychological Concepts

Anchoring Bias: The tendency to rely too heavily on the first piece of information (the "anchor") when making decisions, such as an initial price or estimate.

Cognitive Dissonance: The mental discomfort caused by holding conflicting thoughts or making choices that clash with one's beliefs or expectations.

Endowment Effect: The habit of overvaluing something simply because we own it.

Framing Effect: How information is presented influences decisions, even when the facts remain the same.

Heuristic Thinking: Quick, intuitive decision-making using mental shortcuts rather than full analysis.

Hedonic Adaptation: The tendency to quickly return to a baseline level of satisfaction after positive or negative changes.

Loss Aversion: The fear of losses that makes people more cautious than necessary, often outweighing the motivation for gains.

Perception Bias: The influence of first impressions or appearances on our judgment of people, properties, or opportunities.

Scarcity Mindset: The sense that resources or opportunities are limited, leading to urgency or fear of missing out.

Social Proof: The influence of others' actions or opinions on our own decisions, such as following trends or market behavior.

Status Quo Bias: A preference for maintaining current conditions rather than embracing change, even when change may be beneficial.

Sunk Cost Fallacy: Continuing with a failing decision because of time or money already invested.

Trust Building: The process of creating confidence through honesty, reliability, and transparency in relationships and transactions.

Glossary of Real Estate Concepts

Absorption Rate: The speed at which available properties are sold or leased in a given market during a specific period.

Anchor Tenant: A major or well-known tenant in a commercial property that attracts additional tenants and customers.

Appraisal / Valuation: A professional estimate of a property's market value, used for sales, financing, and investment analysis.

Capitalisation Rate (Cap Rate): The ratio between a property's annual net operating income and its market value. Commonly used to assess investment returns.

Cash Flow: The net amount of income generated by a property after operating expenses and debt service.

Commercial Real Estate (CRE): Properties used for business purposes, including offices, retail centers, warehouses, and industrial spaces.

Comparable Sales (Comps): Recently sold properties with similar characteristics used to estimate market value.

Due Diligence: The process of verifying all material facts about a property before completing a transaction.

Gross Leasable Area (GLA): The total floor area available for tenant occupancy in a commercial property.

Landlord (Lessor): The owner who leases property to a tenant.

Lease Agreement: A legal contract specifying terms, duration, and obligations between a landlord and a tenant.

Maintenance Reserve: Funds set aside for future repairs and upkeep of a property.

Market Value: The estimated price a property would achieve under normal market conditions.

Mixed-Use Development: A property that combines residential, commercial, and sometimes retail or hospitality uses in one project.

Net Operating Income (NOI): The property's income after operating expenses but before debt service and taxes.

Property Manager: The person or company responsible for daily operations, tenant relations, and maintenance of a property.

Residential Real Estate: Properties used for living purposes, including houses, apartments, and multi-family buildings.

Tenant (Lessee): A person or entity who occupies or rents property under a lease agreement.

Vacancy Rate: The percentage of all available units or spaces that are unoccupied at a given time.

Yield: The return on investment generated from a property, typically expressed as a percentage of its cost or market value.

READERS NOTES

Updated List of Books to Date

Willem Tait is the author of several impactful real estate books that examine the dynamic and ever-changing nature of the real estate market. Each book provides valuable strategies, practical insights, and a comprehensive understanding of the key factors influencing the industry. Below is the full list of his published works to date:

Real Estate Law Essentials:
Navigate Cross-Sections, Avoid Pitfalls, and Seize Opportunities. A comprehensive guide to understanding the legal frameworks surrounding real estate, offering practical advice for navigating transactions and mitigating risks.

Proven Principles of Residential Real Estate Investment:
Strategies and Tasks for Building Generational Wealth. A detailed exploration of residential real estate investment strategies, designed to help readers achieve long-term financial security and success.

Practical Principles of Commercial Real Estate Investment:
Tasks and Strategies for Real Estate Success. Focused on commercial real estate, this book provides actionable principles and strategies for navigating the complexities of the market and achieving professional growth.

Real Estate Economics: Property Market Principles and Practices.
This book offers an informative, in-depth analysis of real estate markets, their practices and their underlying principles, and the economic forces driving them.

Raising Money for Real Estate Investment:
Close Deals, Raise Money, Build Wealth. A practical guide to securing funding for real estate projects, this book emphasizes effective deal-making and wealth-building strategies.

Capital Markets and Real Estate:
Bridging Markets for a Global Future. This work explores the intersection of real estate and capital markets, highlighting their convergence and the opportunities that globalization presents for industry professionals.

Real Estate Development and Deal Making:
The Essential Guide for Property Developers, Entrepreneurs, and Dealmakers. This comprehensive guide ties together the foundational principles of property development with innovative strategies for deal-making and entrepreneurship, providing actionable insights for success in the industry.

Psychology of Residential and Commercial Real Estate:
Master the Psychology Behind Real Estate Success. A practical guide into real estate decision making. By uncovering the emotions, motivations, and cognitive biases behind property decisions, this book provides actionable strategies for property success.

Philosophy of Residential and Commercial Real Estate:
Exploring the Intersection of Philosophy, People, Property, Purpose and Spaces. A thoughtful exploration of the deeper meaning behind property and spaces. By examining the beliefs, values, and purposes that shape real estate, this book provides insightful principles for aligning property decisions with vision and intent.

Economics of Banking and Money:
Explores how money and banking shape modern economies. From currency's origins to digital finance, it demystifies complex topics and connects them to daily life. An essential guide for students and curious readers, it shows how trust and innovation drive finance.

Real Estate Mastery Books Series

These books are part of the Real Estate Mastery Books, a series designed to equip readers with the tools and knowledge necessary to excel in the fields of real estate and capital markets. This ever-expanding series reflects Willem Tait's commitment to providing actionable insights and strategies. Keep an eye out for upcoming titles in this growing collection, as there are always more exciting additions to come.

Acknowledgement

This book is the result of years of collaboration, and I owe a great deal of gratitude to the incredible professionals who have shaped my journey in real estate psychology.

To my colleagues, brokers, and agents, thank you for sharing your practical wisdom and experiences that have deepened my understanding of this dynamic industry. Your dedication and expertise have been invaluable.

To the town planners, engineers, architects, and quantity surveyors, your ability to transform concepts into realities has been both inspiring and educational. Your work is a cornerstone of this field and has greatly influenced my perspective.

To landlords and property owners, your stewardship of assets has shown me the importance of resilience and adaptability in an ever-changing market.

To tenants and the businesses they represent, your innovation and collaboration breathe life into real estate, creating thriving communities and opportunities.

To the property developers, contractors, and suppliers, your ability to deliver projects with precision and quality has been an inspiration, underscoring the importance of excellence in execution.

To the attorneys, financiers, and capital market specialists, your insights into property transactions and market trends have broadened my perspective and provided invaluable lessons in strategy and foresight.

This book reflects the collective expertise, vision, and dedication of these professionals. Your influence has enriched this work and inspired my exploration of real estate psychology. For that, I am profoundly grateful.

Willem Tait

Author Bio

Willem Tait is a prolific author, mentor, and consultant with a passion for empowering individuals to thrive both personally and professionally.

As the author of multiple books, Willem combines decades of expertise in real estate, property development, capital markets, law, and venture and equity capital to deliver relatable, actionable guidance that inspires results.

Willem's professional journey is rooted in a deep understanding of the challenges people face in business and life. He offers tools and insights drawn from his wealth of experience to help readers navigate complexities and achieve success with confidence.

A lifelong learner, Willem holds online qualifications in law, real estate, business, psychology, economics, management, and fitness from prestigious institutions such as Yale, Duke, Wharton, Columbia, Penn State, UCI, UC Davis, Case Western, and Johns Hopkins universities. His academic breadth complements his hands-on expertise, making him a trusted resource for readers seeking clarity and practical strategies.

When not writing or consulting, Willem prioritizes balance and well-being through fitness and sports.

His approachable style reflects his dedication to fostering meaningful connections.

Readers can engage with Willem on LinkedIn, Twitter, or via Zoom and Google Meet for thought-provoking advice and engaging discussions.

Social Profiles and Contact Info

Willem Tait is committed to staying connected and engaging with his readers. He is active on LinkedIn and X (formerly Twitter), where he shares updates on his latest projects, insights, and resources.

Willem is also available for face-to-face consultations, public speaking, and group training sessions through platforms like WhatsApp, Zoom, Google Meet, and Microsoft Teams.

Feel free to reach out on any of these platforms to connect, share ideas, or discuss opportunities for learning and growth. Let's keep building together

Email: willemtait@outlook.com

Email: willemtait@gmail.com

Amazon Author:

https://www.amazon.com/author/willemtait

Goodreads: https://www.goodreads.com/willemtait

Linktree: https://linktr.ee/willemtait

Calendly https://calendly.com/willemtait

Linkedin: https://www.linkedin.com/in/willemtait

X: https://x.com/willemtait

Reddit: https://www.reddit.com/user/WillemTait/

Blogger: https://willemtaitauthor.blogspot.com/

Substack: https://willemtait.substack.com/

Medium: https://willemtaitblog.medium.com/

Pinterest: https://.pinterest.com/willemtait/

Public Speaking, Mentorship, Consulting and Coaching

As a dedicated professional with a passion for real estate, business, law, and economics, I thrive on sharing actionable insights and practical strategies that empower individuals and teams to achieve their goals. My expertise spans real estate investment, business consulting, personal growth, and the intricate connections between legal and economic frameworks, allowing me to offer a well-rounded perspective tailored to diverse challenges and ambitions.

Through public speaking engagements, customised mentorship programs, and dynamic one-on-one or group coaching sessions, I aim to inspire, educate, and guide.

Whether addressing an audience of hundreds or working closely with a small team, my mission is to deliver value-driven insights that leave a lasting impact.

If you're seeking a keynote speaker to energise and inform your event, a consultant to elevate your business strategies, or a mentor to foster personal and professional growth, I'm here to collaborate.

My approach integrates years of hands-on experience with a solid foundation in real estate, law and economics, ensuring the strategies I share are both practical and informed by robust principles.

Let's connect to explore how I can help you or your organisation unlock new opportunities and achieve meaningful success.

Together, we can create strategies that inspire growth, drive innovation, and deliver measurable results.

LinkedIn: https://www.linkedin.com/in/willemtait/

Mail: willemtait@outlook.com

Upcoming Projects

Thank you for joining me on this journey into the fascinating world of real estate.

This book represents just one part of a larger series designed to guide you through the strategies, insights, and opportunities that shape the real estate industry.

Real estate is a field of limitless potential, where knowledge and preparation are the keys to unlocking success.

Through this series, I aim to provide you with the tools, understanding, and confidence to navigate its complexities and seize its opportunities.

Each book in the series builds on the knowledge shared here, diving deeper into critical topics like advanced investment strategies, property development, market trends, and innovative funding solutions.

While this book lays the groundwork, the subsequent works take a closer look at specific challenges and opportunities, empowering you to make informed decisions and create a thriving portfolio.

By exploring these additional books, you can enhance your expertise and develop a well-rounded perspective on what it takes to succeed in real estate.

What sets this series apart is its focus on practicality and applicability.

Backed by extensive research and enriched with real-world case studies, these books offer actionable advice that you can immediately apply to your ventures.

From understanding market dynamics to mastering the art of negotiation and scaling your investments, each installment provides a roadmap for achieving your goals.

I encourage you to continue your journey by exploring the other books in this series.

Whether you are new to real estate or a seasoned investor, the insights and strategies presented across these works are designed to meet you where you are and help you grow.

Together, these books form a comprehensive toolkit to support your success in this ever-evolving field.

I hope that this series will not only provide you with the knowledge and strategies you need but also inspire you to think bigger, act boldly, and pursue opportunities with confidence.

The real estate industry is dynamic, rewarding, and full of potential, and I am honored to be a part of your learning process.

Thank you for choosing to explore this series, and I look forward to continuing this journey with you in many more pages.

We Value Your Feedback!

Your thoughts and opinions mean the world to me. I wrote this book with the goal of providing you with valuable insights and practical strategies for raising money for real estate investment.

However, I know every reader's experience is unique, and your feedback helps me understand what worked well for you and what I can improve. It's through your input that I can continue to refine my work and make future books even more impactful.

Whether you found this book incredibly helpful, thought-provoking, or feel there's room for improvement, I'd love to hear from you. Every comment, suggestion, or review helps me grow and deliver better content to meet your needs.

Think of this as a collaboration, your feedback directly shapes the tools and resources I create for readers like you.

If you have a moment, I'd be grateful if you could leave a review on Amazon or your favorite platform. Your thoughts not only help me improve but also guide other readers who are searching for practical resources in real estate investment.

Thank you for taking the time to share your experience. Your voice truly makes a difference, and it inspires me to keep creating content that serves and empowers.

Blessings and best wishes.

Willem Tait

READERS NOTES

READERS NOTES

READERS NOTES

READERS NOTES

READERS NOTES

Portfolio of Books by Willem Tait

For more, kindly see www.amazon.com/author/willemtait

BUSINESS AND REAL ESTATE BOOKS

1. **Real Estate Law Essentials:** Navigate Cross-Sections, Avoid Pitfalls, and Seize Opportunities.
2. **Proven Principles of Residential Real Estate Investment:** Strategies and Tasks for Building Generational Wealth.
3. **Practical Principles of Commercial Real Estate Investment:** Tasks and Strategies for Real Estate Success.
4. **Real Estate Economics:** Property Market Principles and Practices.
5. **Raising Money for Real Estate Investment:** Close Deals, Raise Money, Build Wealth.
6. **Capital Markets and Real Estate:** How Money and Capital Shapes the Property Market.
7. **Real Estate Development and Deal Making:** The Essential Guide for Property Developers, Entrepreneurs, and Dealmakers.
8. **Psychology of Residential and Commercial Real Estate:** Master the Psychology Behind Real Estate Success.
9. **Philosophy of Residential and Commercial Real Estate:** Exploring the Intersection of Philosophy, People, Property, Purpose and Spaces.
10. **Economics of Banking and Money:** Insight into Power, Trust, and Change.
11. **The Future of Real Estate:** PropTech, Sustainability and Design

SELF-HELP AND MOTIVATIONAL BOOKS

1. **Sort Your Crap Out:** Own Your Choices, Silence Your Critic. Get Stuff Done
2. **Dammit, Get It Together:** Stop Making Excuses and Start Living the Life You Deserve
3. **Stop Giving a Damn and Start Living:** Cut the Crap. Focus on What Matters. Live Fully
4. **Dammit, It's Your Life:** Own Your Mind, Time, and Choices
5. **Dammit, Stop Being Overwhelmed and Overworked:** Reclaim Your Time, Energy, and Sanity

ANNOTATED AND COMMENTARY

1. **The Way to Wealth** (Annotated): With Motivational Commentary by Willem Tait
2. **The Art Of War:** (Annotated): Proven Modern Strategies for Winning in Business, Leadership, and Life by Willem Tait

www.ingramcontent.com/pod-product-compliance
Lightning Source LLC
Chambersburg PA
CBHW071552220526

45469CB00003B/990